To Sue Sue —
I hope this book inspires you in the kitchen. Thank you for all of your support.

Nicole Putzel

THE *seasoned* PLATE

DELICIOUS AND HEALTHY

REAL FOOD

RECIPES BY THE SEASON

NICOLE PUTZEL

PHOTOGRAPHED BY: CLAUDIA CHOCANO

Putzel Kitchen LLC
www.putzelkitchen.com
nicole@putzelkitchen.com

About this Book

This cookbook is the result of a beautiful recipe: one of food, friendship, and wellness, told by the seasons.

Nicole and Claudia first met when their now-teenage boys were in preschool. Years into their friendship, during a trip to the local farmers' market, they started discussing their current projects and contemplated the possibility of collaborating on a food photography enterprise. Ultimately, they decided to create a cookbook together—this very book.

The story went like this: For about a year, Nicole would create a seasonal, vegetable-centric recipe every Friday, and during the summer months, the produce for the recipes was literally harvested from her backyard—truly, organic-garden-to-plate dining.

The two women then styled the food in its true edible form—no tricks—and once they were satisfied with the visual appeal, Claudia photographed the dishes in natural, seasonal light. Once the photos had been taken, they sat at the kitchen table and consumed the fruits of their labors. After all, what can possibly be better than breaking bread with friends?

These are the delicious dishes that they enjoyed. They hope you gather around your kitchen table to devour them with loved ones, too.

Dedication

For Steve, Jake, and Natalie, who are my most honest taste testers.

For my mom Jacki, who introduced me to the artistic and flavorful wonders of cooking.

For Ollie, who always keeps me company in the kitchen.

Nicole

For my boys, Ignacio and Alejandro, hoping that one day, they will eat this healthy.

Claudia

Table of Contents

Fall

Kale + Beet Greens Salad

Prep
30 m

Yield
4 servings

Kale is a hearty staple in our house, as it's one of the first crops to spring up in my garden and also usually the last one standing in the fall. We did our first photo shoot for the book with this garden-to-plate salad made from our harvest that same lovely fall day.

ingredients

for the dressing
(makes about ¾ cup)

½ cup olive oil

¼ cup white wine vinegar

1 tablespoon chopped fresh
    tarragon leaves

1 teaspoon Dijon mustard

½ teaspoon sea salt

½ teaspoon freshly ground
    black pepper

for the salad

1 beet, greens (leaves) attached

1 bunch kale, ribs removed and
    finely chopped (about 4 cups)

1 Honey Crisp apple, thinly sliced

2 carrots, peeled and chopped

2 celery stalks, diced

½ cup chopped fresh flat-leaf
    parsley

½ cup lightly chopped fresh dill
    fronds

2 tablespoons pine nuts, toasted,
    for garnish

¼ cup crumbled goat cheese,
    for garnish (optional)

method

1. Make dressing: Whisk together olive oil, white wine vinegar, tarragon, mustard, sea salt, and black pepper until emulsified.
2. Make salad: Peel beet; remove and reserve greens (leaves).
3. Using a vegetable spiralizer or similar tool, make "boodles" (beet noodles).
4. Chiffonade beet greens by rolling leaves together tightly and thinly slicing.
5. Assemble salad if serving immediately by tossing kale and beet greens together with dressing in bowl until all leaves are lightly coated. Top with boodles, apple, carrots, celery, parsley, and dill.
6. Garnish with pine nuts and goat cheese, if using, and serve.

take a short cut: Prepare all salad ingredients, other than dill, in advance. Mix dressing in glass jar with lid. Massage kale and beet greens with 2 tablespoons of dressing. Dress and garnish salad with remaining dressing just prior to serving.

Farro Salad with Orange + Pomegranate

Prep
20 m

Yield
8 servings

I love how the chewy texture of the farro in this salad contrasts with the crunch of the pomegranate arils and celery. The flavors are a good complement to any meal, but the salad is hearty enough to be a meal itself.

ingredients

1 orange
¼ cup olive oil
¼ cup balsamic vinegar
¼ teaspoon sea salt + more, to taste
¼ teaspoon freshly ground black pepper + more, to taste
1 pomegranate
2 cups farro, cooked al dente per instructions on package
    (I like Trader Joe's 10 Minute Farro)
2 cups arugula
2 celery ribs, chopped
¼ cup chopped pecans, toasted
¼ cup finely chopped fresh dill fronds, for garnish
1 tablespoon crumbled goat cheese, for garnish

method

1. Zest orange and reserve zest in Mason jar. Peel and segment orange and set fruit aside for salad.
2. Combine olive oil, balsamic vinegar, ¼ teaspoon sea salt, ¼ teaspoon black pepper, and orange zest in Mason jar. Tightly fasten lid and shake until dressing is emulsified.
3. Slice pomegranate in half. Fill bowl with water and place each pomegranate half face down in water. Firmly tap skin side of fruit until arils (little red jewels) fall into water (water helps keep the red juice from squirting everywhere!). Pick out arils from remaining pith and remove from water. Set aside in small bowl.
4. Combine farro, celery, orange segments, pomegranate arils, and pecans in large bowl. Drizzle with dressing and gently toss until all ingredients completely combine.
5. Season with sea salt and black pepper to taste.
6. Garnish with dill and goat cheese and serve.

Kale Salad-in-a-Jar with Carrot-Ginger-Miso Dressing

Prep
30 m

Yield
4 servings

The layers of color in this salad—the orange of the carrot dressing, the greens of the kale and celery, the purple of the cabbage, and the red of the peppers—make it look like a rainbow in a jar. It's the perfect presentation if you're planning to bring a small salad to a dinner party. The dressing ends up pouring over the salad as you empty the jar into a bowl for serving.

ingredients

for the dressing (makes 2 cups)

3 carrots, peeled and chopped (about 1 cup)

½ cup grapeseed oil

¼ cup rice wine vinegar

½ cup freshly squeezed orange juice (more for thinner dressing)

1 (4-inch) piece fresh ginger, peeled and chopped (about ¼ cup)

3 tablespoons white or yellow miso paste

1 tablespoon toasted sesame oil

Few pinches freshly ground black pepper

for the salad

1 bunch kale, ribs removed and finely chopped (about 4 cups)

3 celery stalks, thinly sliced

¼ head purple cabbage, shredded

1 red bell pepper, julienned (thinly sliced)

1 carrot, peeled and ribboned

2 tablespoons crumbled goat cheese

2 tablespoons chopped pecans, toasted, for garnish

method

1. Make dressing: Combine all dressing ingredients in powerful blender and puree until smooth.
2. Pour dressing into bottom of large (½-gallon) Mason jar.
3. Make salad: Starting with kale, layer each salad ingredient except pecans, one by one, in Mason jar. (Reserve pecans until serving because they soften in refrigerator.) Cover jar with tight-fitting lid and refrigerate up to 2 days.
4. Empty contents of jar into large serving bowl, add pecans, and toss. Serve.

Grilled Rainbow trout

Prep
5 m

Cook
10 m

Yield
4 servings

Rainbow trout is a delicate fish, so it cooks quickly. Since its mild flavor makes this fish appealing to even the pickiest eater, and it can be prepared on the grill or in the oven, this fast, well-balanced entrée is a welcome addition to any busy person's meal repertoire.

ingredients

4 lemons

Aluminum foil

4 whole rainbow trout, heads on, butterflied, and filleted

1 teaspoon large flake sea salt

1 teaspoon freshly ground black pepper

¼ cup Newman's Own Classic Oil and Vinegar dressing

½ cup roughly chopped fresh flat-leaf parsley, for garnish

method

1. Cut 2 lemons into thin slices. Cut other two lemons in half. Set aside.
2. If roasting in oven, preheat oven to 400°F; if grilling, heat grill to medium-high (about 400°F).
3. Line 2 rimmed baking sheets with aluminum foil. Place 2 fish on each baking sheet, scale side down, so each is open like a book. Season each fish with ¼ teaspoon each sea salt and black pepper. Pour 1 tablespoon dressing over each fish and top with thin lemon slices.
4. Roast in oven 10 minutes or grill, open faced on double sheets of foil, 5-6 minutes. Remove from heat.
5. Squeeze ½ lemon over each fish, garnish with parsley, and serve.

Basic Tomato Sauce

Prep
15 m

Cook
50 m

Yield
2 quarts

This basic tomato sauce is a staple in my kitchen, and the flavor is anything but basic. Since the recipe yields more than I usually need, I freeze the leftovers to have on hand when in a pinch.

ingredients

2 tablespoons olive oil

1 onion, chopped

4 carrots, peeled and chopped

4 celery stalks, chopped

4 garlic cloves, minced

2 teaspoons sea salt + more, as needed

2 teaspoons freshly ground black pepper + more, as needed

1 teaspoon dried basil

1 teaspoon dried oregano

½ teaspoon crushed red pepper

6½ cups chopped fresh tomatoes or 2 (28-ounce) cans chopped San Marzano tomatoes

1 bay leaf

1 tablespoon balsamic vinegar

Handful fresh basil leaves, very thinly sliced, for garnish

method

1. In saucepan over low-medium heat, warm olive oil until wavy. Add onion and sauté, stirring frequently, 10 minutes, or until translucent.
2. Add carrots and celery increase heat to medium and sauté 3 minutes. Add garlic, 2 teaspoons each sea salt and black pepper, dried basil, dried oregano, and crushed red pepper and sauté, stirring continuously, 3 to 4 minutes.
3. Add tomatoes and bay leaf, increase heat to medium-high and bring to a simmer. Let simmer about 30 minutes. Remove from heat.
4. Remove and discard bay leaf. Use immersion blender or transfer sauce in batches to jug of a powerful blender to puree until smooth (if using blender, then return to saucepan).
5. Add balsamic vinegar and taste to check seasoning; add more sea salt and black pepper as needed. Garnish with fresh basil and serve.

take a shortcut: Sauce can be made 2 to 3 days ahead. If making a big batch, freeze in small portions so it's easy to defrost as needed.

think out of the icebox: Use mushrooms instead of onion and add any leftover vegetables from last night's dinner.

Autumn Root Vegetable Salad

Prep
20 m

Yield
4 servings

The combination of fennel, apples, and celery makes this salad crunchy and sweet, and it's counterbalanced by the tartness of the mustard vinaigrette. I like to drizzle some balsamic glaze over it for a fancy finish that wows my guests.

ingredients

**for the dressing
(makes about ½ cup)**

¼ cup olive oil

2 tablespoons red wine vinegar

1½ teaspoons Dijon mustard

1 teaspoon chopped fresh
   tarragon leaves

½ teaspoon sea salt

½ teaspoon freshly ground
   black pepper

for the salad

4 celery stalks, chopped

1 fennel bulb, thinly sliced

½ red apple, thinly sliced

½ green apple, thinly sliced

½ cup chopped fresh flat-leaf
   parsley (about 1 bunch)

½ cup Trader Joe's candied
   pecans, for topping

1 tablespoon balsamic glaze, for
   drizzling

method

1. Make dressing: Whisk together olive oil, red wine vinegar, Dijon mustard, tarragon, sea salt, and black pepper until emulsified.
2. Make salad: Combine celery, fennel, apples, and parsley in a serving bowl and toss with dressing. Top with candied pecans, drizzle with balsamic glaze, and serve.

note: Slice the extra apple halves for use as garnish if you don't eat them while preparing salad.

Autumn Apple Beet Salad

Prep
10 m

Yield
4 servings

This is another twist on the Autumn Root Vegetable Salad (see previous recipe). The addition of caramelized beets with lavender gives the salad a distinct flavor which allows for a simple balsamic and olive oil finish.

ingredients

1 (5-ounce) package baby kale

1 cup beets from Caramelized Beets with Honey'd Lavender Ricotta recipe (see p. 105)

½ red apple, thinly sliced

½ green apple, thinly sliced

½ cup finely chopped fresh flat-leaf parsley

¼ cup pecan halves

3 tablespoons crumbled goat cheese

Fennel fronds, for garnish and flavor

Sea salt, to taste

Freshly ground black pepper, to taste

Balsamic glaze, for drizzling

Olive oil, for drizzling

method

1. Place kale in large serving bowl and top with beets, apples, parsley, pecans, and goat cheese. Garnish with fennel fronds.

2. Divide salad among 4 serving plates and season each serving with pinch each of sea salt and freshly ground black pepper. Dress servings with few drizzles each of balsamic glaze and olive oil to taste just before serving. Serve.

Cinnamon-Vanilla Applesauce

Prep
10 m

Cook
20 m

Yield
2 quarts

Homemade applesauce is healthy comfort food: sweet, soft, and smooth. Combine different types of apples, since some varieties are tart and crisp and others are sweet and soft. I like to leave the skin on about half the apples to add to the color of the applesauce.

ingredients

6 Cortland apples, cored and cubed (about 6 cups)

6 Honey Crisp apples, peeled, cored, and cubed (about 6 cups)

1 cup water + more, as needed

1 vanilla bean, whole

1 cinnamon stick

method

1. Combine all ingredients in saucepan over medium-low heat and cook, stirring every few minutes, until apples are mushy. Add more water if needed. Remove from heat.

2. Remove and discard cinnamon stick. Remove vanilla bean, slice lengthwise, and scrape seeds from pod. Discard pod.

3. Combine apple mixture and vanilla seeds in jug of a powerful blender and puree until smooth; add more water if needed. Serve warm or chilled.

Ratatouille with Individual Polenta Cakes

Prep
30 m

Cook
50 m

Yield
8 servings

Ratatouille is a Provençal vegetable stew featuring eggplant and tomatoes as its main ingredients. The grilled eggplant in this recipe cuts down its overall cooking time and adds a unique, smoky flavor.

ingredients

1 large eggplant, sliced into rounds

1½ teaspoons fine sea salt, for degorging eggplant

Grapeseed oil, for oiling grill

2 tablespoons olive oil

1 yellow onion, cut into small dice

1 zucchini squash, cut into medium dice

1 yellow squash, cut into medium dice

1 red bell pepper, cut into medium dice

1 yellow bell pepper, cut into medium dice

1 orange bell pepper, cut into medium dice

4 garlic cloves, minced

1 teaspoon dried basil

1 teaspoon dried oregano

1 teaspoon sea salt

1 teaspoon freshly ground black pepper

1 (28-ounce) can chopped San Marzano tomatoes with juice

⅓ cup chopped fresh basil leaves

2 tablespoons chopped fresh oregano

Individual Polenta Cakes (see recipe on p. 27), for serving

method

1. Degorge liquid from eggplant by sprinkling each slice with few pinches fine sea salt and set aside 10-12 minutes. (Note: It will appear as though the eggplant is perspiring.) Wipe off salt and water and repeat on other side.

2. Preheat grill to medium-high heat (about 400°F). Lightly oil eggplant rounds with grapeseed oil. Rub hot grill grates with rag dipped in grapeseed oil. Place eggplant rounds on hot grill and grill each side about 5 minutes, or until golden brown with grill marks. Remove from grill and set aside to cool.

3. Once cooled, cut eggplant into small pieces and set aside.

recipe continues on p. 26

Ratatouille with Individual Polenta Cakes *continued*

method *continued*

4. In saucepan over medium-low heat, warm 2 tablespoons olive oil until wavy. Add onion and sauté, stirring frequently, 10 minutes, or until translucent.
5. Add zucchini, yellow squash, and bell peppers and increase to medium heat. Sauté 10 minutes, and add garlic, dried basil, dried oregano, sea salt, and black pepper stirring continuously, 2 minutes.
6. Add tomatoes with juice and grilled eggplant and bring to simmer and cover. Let simmer covered about 20 minutes. Remove from heat.
7. Top with fresh basil and oregano and serve with Polenta Cakes.

Individual Polenta Cakes

Prep
5 m

Cook
40-45 m

Yield
12 cakes

ingredients

Nonstick cooking spray

Aluminum foil baking cups

2 tablespoons olive oil

2 tablespoons unsalted butter

1 shallot, finely chopped

1 quart chicken or vegetable stock

1 cup corn meal

¾ cup freshly grated parmesan cheese

1½ teaspoons sea salt

1 teaspoon freshly ground black pepper

method

1. Preheat oven to 375°F. Grease 12-cup muffin pan with nonstick cooking spray and line with aluminum foil baking cups.

2. In medium pot over low heat, melt together olive oil and butter. Add shallot and sauté, stirring frequently, 5 minutes, or until translucent and lightly golden.

3. Add stock and bring to simmer. Gradually add corn meal, ¼ cup at a time, and simmer, whisking continuously to avoid lumps, 10 minutes. Remove from heat and stir in parmesan cheese, sea salt, and black pepper.

4. Pour about ½ cup of mixture into each prepared baking cup and bake 25 minutes. Check for doneness with toothpick; return to oven and continue baking if toothpick does not come out clean. Remove from oven.

Curried Cauliflower with Cilantro, Almonds, + Golden Raisins

Prep
10 m

Cook
15 m

Yield
4 servings

Sweet raisins are an unexpected surprise in this curried cauliflower dish, and the yellow curry and green cilantro look beautiful together in a serving bowl.

ingredients

1 head cauliflower, cut into florets

1 tablespoon olive oil

1 tablespoon curry powder

¼ teaspoon sea salt

3 tablespoons vegan mayonnaise (Vegenaise) or regular mayonnaise

Freshly grated zest and freshly squeezed juice of 1 lime

¼ cup chopped fresh cilantro leaves

¼ cup yellow raisins

¼ cup sliced almonds

method

1. Preheat oven to 400°F.

2. Toss cauliflower florets in bowl with olive oil, curry powder, and sea salt. Transfer florets to baking sheet and roast in oven 15 minutes. Remove from oven and let cool.

3. While cauliflower cools, whisk together mayonnaise, lime zest, and lime juice. Add to cauliflower and toss until completely coated.

4. Stir in cilantro, raisins, and almonds and serve at room temperature.

Shaved Brussels Sprouts with Roasted Squash, Pomegranate, + Parsley

Prep
15 m

Cook
25 m

Yield
6-8 servings

Brussels sprouts make a great base for a fall salad and can be served either raw or sautéed. I really like the sweet, crunchy pomegranate arils mixed with the shaved sprouts in this recipe.

ingredients

¼ cup date syrup

¼ cup coconut oil (melted if you have the solid form)

1 tablespoon ground cinnamon

2 acorn squash, seeded, peeled, and cut into eighths

3–4 cups shredded Brussels sprouts (about 1 pound)

2 tablespoons olive oil

2 tablespoons white balsamic vinegar

½ teaspoon sea salt

½ teaspoon freshly ground black pepper

Arils of 1 pomegranate

1 bunch fresh flat-leaf parsley, finely chopped, for garnish

Shaved parmesan cheese, for garnish (optional)

Balsamic glaze, for drizzling (optional)

method

1. Preheat oven to 400°F and line rimmed baking sheet with parchment paper. If roasting Brussels sprouts, line another rimmed baking sheet with parchment paper.

2. Whisk together date syrup, coconut oil, and cinnamon. Place squash in bowl, drizzle on date syrup mixture, and toss well. Transfer squash to prepared baking sheet and roast 25 minutes. Remove from oven.

3. If roasting Brussels sprouts, toss in bowl with olive oil until very lightly dressed and season with sea salt and black pepper. Transfer to prepared baking sheet and roast 20 minutes or until golden brown (you can roast at the same time as the squash). Remove from oven and transfer to bowl. Add white balsamic vinegar and toss.

4. If serving Brussels sprouts raw, simply toss with olive oil and white vinegar and season with sea salt and black pepper.

5. Layer roasted or raw Brussels sprouts on a platter. Top with roasted squash, pomegranate arils and parsley. Garnish with parmesan shavings and drizzle with balsamic glaze, if using, and serve.

Turkey-Bison Meatballs with Zoodles + Roasted Tomatoes

Prep
10 m

Cook
30 m

Yield
2 dozen meatballs

This recipe is a great way to cut back on starchy carbs while still achieving vibrant flavor and a variety of textures. If you aren't a Zoodle fan, the meatballs also pair well with traditional pasta, rice, or ratatouille. The meatballs freeze well, too.

ingredients

1 tablespoon olive oil

1 onion, finely chopped

2 garlic cloves, minced

1 teaspoon dried oregano

1 teaspoon dried basil

1 teaspoon sea salt

½ teaspoon freshly ground
    black pepper

1 pound ground turkey
    (dark meat only)

1 pound ground bison

1 cup cooked quinoa

2 whole large eggs

1 tablespoon + 1 teaspoon
    tomato paste

1 recipe Zoodles (recipe
    follows on next page)

1 recipe Balsamic Roasted
    Tomatoes (recipe follows
    on p. 34)

Freshly grated parmesan
    cheese, for topping (op-
    tional)

method

1. In sauté pan over low-medium heat, warm olive oil until wavy. Add onion and sauté, stirring frequently, 10 minutes, or until translucent and lightly golden.

2. Add garlic, oregano, basil, salt, and black pepper and sauté 2 minutes. Remove from heat and let cool.

3. Preheat oven to 400°F and line rimmed baking sheet with foil.

4. Combine turkey and bison meat in large bowl and add cooled onion mixture, quinoa, eggs, and tomato paste. Mix until well combined.

5. Form turkey–bison mixture into 24 golf ball-sized meatballs and space evenly on prepared baking sheet.

6. Bake 20 minutes, or until internal temperature of meatballs reaches 165°F. Remove from oven.

7. Serve hot with Zoodles and Balsamic Roasted Tomatoes. Top the Zoodles with parmesan cheese, if using.

Zoodles

Prep
3 m

Cook
2 m

Yield
4 servings

ingredients

2 large zucchini squash

2 tablespoons olive oil

Pinch sea salt

Few grinds freshly ground black pepper

method

1. Using a vegetable spiralizer or similar tool, make "zoodles" (zucchini noodles).

2. In large sauté pan over medium-high heat, warm 1 tablespoon olive oil. Add half the zoodles and sauté about 2 minutes. Remove to platter and repeat with remaining zoodles. Remove from heat and season with sea salt and black pepper. Serve.

Balsamic Roasted Tomatoes

Prep
10 m

Cook
20 m

Yield
4 servings

ingredients

1 pound cherry tomatoes, halved (about 3 cups)

4 garlic cloves, minced

2 tablespoons olive oil

1 tablespoon oregano white balsamic vinegar (available at oil and vinegar shops or online)

1/4 teaspoon sea salt

1/4 teaspoon freshly ground black pepper

method

1. Preheat oven to 450°F and line rimmed baking sheet with parchment paper.
2. Mix all ingredients together in a bowl.
3. Transfer to prepared baking sheet and roast 20 minutes. Remove from oven.

Winter

Eggy Avocado Toast

Prep
5 m

Cook
5 m

Yield
1 serving

This avocado toast is a complete meal in minutes. The egg adds a protein dimension to this dish that can be eaten for breakfast, lunch, or dinner. I love to make this with a sunny side-up egg with a runny yolk and soak the yolk up with the toasted bread.

ingredients

1 slice whole grain bread

¼ avocado, sliced

Few pinches sea salt

Freshly squeezed juice of ¼ lime

½ cup arugula leaves

1 slice cheddar cheese

1 whole large egg

method

1. Toast bread.
2. Spread avocado slices on top of bread. Sprinkle with sea salt and squeeze lime juice over avocado.
3. Layer avocado toast with arugula and cheese.
4. Poach or fry egg. Remove from heat.
5. Slide cooked egg on top of cheese while still hot, allowing cheese to melt, and serve, or serve deconstructed.

Ginger Soy Salmon

 Prep
10 m + 4 h

 Cook
14 m

 Yield
4 servings

This grilled salmon recipe is simple, but the story where it came from is not. To make a long story short, this recipe was created by my late Uncle Arnie's ex-wife. Although the marriage was brief, the recipe has been a staple in our family for many years now.

ingredients

½ cup grapeseed oil

½ cup tamari soy sauce

Freshly squeezed juice of 1 lemon (about ¼ cup)

1 tablespoon light brown sugar, densely packed

1 tablespoon chopped fresh ginger

1 garlic clove, minced

4 (4-ounce) salmon fillets

method

1. Combine grapeseed oil, tamari soy sauce, brown sugar, lemon juice, ginger, and garlic in a powerful blender and blend until smooth. Transfer contents of blender jug to gallon-size zip-top bag or wide casserole dish, reserving about ¼ cup in sealed glass jar for serving.

2. Place salmon fillets, flesh side down, in marinade. Cover and refrigerate up to 4 hours.

3. Preheat grill to medium-high heat. Lightly oil grill and place fillets on it, flesh side down. Grill 5 to 7 minutes.

4. Using grill spatula, turn fillets over. Fillets should release easily; if not, give a bit more time. Grill on skin side another 5 minutes or so. Once internal temperature of fillets reaches 145°F, remove from grill. If skin sticks to grill, cook a little longer and then remove (crisp grilled skin is delicious and full of good-for-you omega-3 fatty acids). Serve hot with reserved sauce.

think outside the grill (aka an alternative method): If you don't have a grill handy, bake fillets in a 400°F oven 20 to 25 minutes.

Butternut Squash Soup with White Beans + Kale

Prep
20 m

Cook
50 m

Yield
3 quarts

Nothing warms the soul on a chilly winter day like a bowl of soup. The combination of squash, kale, and beans offers a beautiful array of colors, flavor, and texture. Pair the soup with a crusty chunk of bread, and you have a comforting meal.

ingredients

Olive oil, for cooking

1 yellow onion, chopped

4 carrots, peeled and chopped

4 celery stalks, chopped

4 garlic cloves, minced

1 tablespoon chopped fresh rosemary leaves (about 2–3 sprigs)

2 teaspoons dried thyme

2 teaspoons sea salt

2 teaspoons freshly ground black pepper

2 tablespoons tomato paste

2 quarts chicken or vegetable stock

2 cups butternut squash, peeled and cubed into 1-inch pieces

10 ounces (1 bunch) kale, chopped

1 bay leaf

1 parmesan cheese rind

2 (15-ounce) cans white beans, rinsed and drained

Freshly grated parmesan cheese, for garnish

Crusty bread, for serving

method

1. In stockpot over medium-low heat, warm a few tablespoons olive oil until wavy. Add onion and sauté 3–5 minutes. Add carrots and celery and sauté 3 minutes. Add garlic, rosemary, thyme, sea salt, and black pepper and cook, stirring constantly, 2 minutes. Mix in tomato paste.

2. Add stock, squash, kale, and bay leaf, raise heat to medium-high, and bring to a boil.

3. Add cheese rind, reduce heat to low, and simmer 20 minutes, until squash is tender enough to pierce with a fork.

4. Add white beans and simmer 10 minutes. Remove from heat. Remove and discard bay leaf and cheese rind.

5. Transfer to serving bowl. Garnish with parmesan cheese and serve hot with crusty bread.

turkey tacos with Black Beans

Prep
10 m

Cook
35 m

Yield
8 servings

Turkey tacos are on the regular dinner rotation at my house. My daughter's friends love this recipe so much that they've asked me to share it with the lunchroom cooks at school.

ingredients

1 pound ground beef

1 pound ground turkey (dark meat)

1 tablespoon chili powder

1½ teaspoons ground cumin

1 teaspoon sea salt

1 teaspoon freshly ground black pepper

½ teaspoon smoked paprika

¼ teaspoon garlic powder

¼ teaspoon red pepper flakes

¼ teaspoon dried oregano

28 ounces chopped San Marzano tomatoes with juice

1 (15-ounce) can black beans, rinsed and drained

1–2 teaspoons olive oil, for cooking

4 scallions, thinly sliced

Taco shells, shredded lettuce, shredded cheddar or queso fresco cheese, Guacamole, and Cucumber Mango Salsa (see recipes on p. 47), for serving

method

1. In large sauté pan over medium-high heat, mix together and brown ground beef and turkey. Cover and simmer 15 minutes.
2. While meat is cooking, prepare seasoning by mixing together chili powder, cumin, sea salt, black pepper, paprika, garlic powder, red pepper flakes, and oregano in a small glass jar. Set aside.
3. Remove pan from heat and drain fat into heat-safe container. Return pan to medium heat.
4. In small pan over medium heat, warm olive oil. Add scallions and 1 teaspoon seasoning mix and sauté about 5 minutes, or until scallions soften. Remove from heat.
5. Add sautéed scallions and additional 2 tablespoons seasoning mix to meat. Stir in tomatoes with juice, cover, and simmer about 15 minutes.
6. Add black beans and simmer 5 minutes. Remove from heat.
7. Serve hot with taco shells, lettuce, cheese, Guacamole, and Cucumber Mango Salsa.

Cucumber Mango Salsa

Prep
10 m

Yield
8 servings

ingredients

1 mango, peeled and finely diced (about ¾ cup)

½ large cucumber, seeded and finely diced (about 1 cup)

½ red bell pepper, seeded and finely diced

1 jalapeño pepper, seeded and finely diced

Freshly squeezed juice of 1 lime

4 scallions, white parts only, thinly sliced

2 tablespoons finely chopped fresh mint leaves

1 teaspoon sea salt

½ teaspoon freshly ground black pepper

method

1. Mix all ingredients in a bowl. It's *that* easy.

Guacamole

Prep
5 m

Yield
8 servings

ingredients

4 ripe avocados, halved and pitted

1–2 jalapeño peppers, deseeded (the heat is in the seeds) and finely diced

Freshly squeezed juice of 1 lime

2 tablespoons chopped cilantro leaves

1 garlic clove, minced

½ teaspoon sea salt

¼ teaspoon freshly ground black pepper

¼ teaspoon ground cumin (optional)

method

1. Scoop out avocado flesh and smash in a mortar and pestle or in a bowl with a fork. Mix in jalapeños, lime juice, cilantro, and garlic.

2. Season with sea salt, black pepper, and cumin, if using, and serve.

Apple-Stuffed Acorn Squash

Prep
10 m

Cook
1 h

Yield
4 servings

Stuffed acorn squash is one of my favorite comfort foods. It's like a warm and sweet dessert, but it's also healthy enough to serve as a side dish at dinner.

ingredients

2 acorn squash, halved and seeded

1 apple, peeled and chopped

¼ cup brown sugar

¼ cup melted coconut oil

2 teaspoons ground cinnamon

¼ cup chopped walnuts or pecans, toasted

¼ cup raisins

method

1. Preheat oven to 400°F and line baking sheet with foil. Place acorn squash halves on prepared baking sheet. *Note: I like to balance the squash halves on Mason jar lid bands so they don't topple over in the pan.*

2. Combine apples, coconut oil, brown sugar, and cinnamon in a bowl. Stuff each squash half with ¼ cup or more of the apple mixture.

3. Bake 1 hour, until squash halves are fork tender. Remove from oven.

4. Scatter 1 tablespoon each of toasted nuts and raisins over each half and serve warm.

Vegetarian Chili

Prep
15 m

Cook
1 h 10 m

Yield
3 quarts

Vegetarian chili is the ideal dish for a snowy day. It sounds crazy, but the secret ingredient that gives my chili its rich flavor is cacao powder. Cacao is also loaded with antioxidants; this added benefit is among the many nutrients in this healthy comfort food.

ingredients

1 tablespoon olive oil, for cooking

1 yellow onion, chopped

4 garlic cloves, minced

1 orange bell pepper, seeded and chopped

1 red bell pepper, seeded and chopped

1 yellow bell pepper, seeded and chopped

1 jalapeño pepper, seeded and finely diced

1 zucchini, chopped

1 sweet potato, peeled and chopped

2 quarts chicken or vegetable stock

1 (28-ounce) can chopped San Marzano tomatoes, drained

1 tablespoon cacao powder

1 tablespoon chili powder

1 tablespoon ground cumin

2 teaspoons dried basil

2 teaspoons dried oregano

2 teaspoons sea salt + more, as needed

2 teaspoons freshly ground black pepper + more, as needed

3 bay leaves

Pinch red pepper flakes

2 (15-ounce) cans black beans, rinsed and drained

2 (15-ounce) cans red beans, rinsed and drained

1 (15-ounce) can garbanzo beans (chickpeas), rinsed and drained

Chopped fresh cilantro and shredded cheddar cheese, for garnish

method

1. In stockpot over medium-low heat, warm olive oil until wavy. Add onion and sauté 10 minutes. Add garlic and sauté, stirring constantly, 1 minute. Stir in orange, red, yellow, and jalapeño peppers. Stir in zucchini and sweet potato.

2. Add all remaining ingredients except beans, raise heat to medium-high, and bring to a simmer. Simmer 30 minutes.

3. Add beans and simmer 15 to 30 minutes. Remove and discard bay leaves and taste for seasoning; adjust as needed. Remove from heat and serve hot garnished with the cilantro and cheese.

Citrus + Pomegranate Salad with Mint

Prep
20 m

Yield
4 servings

Chef and author Lauren Braun Costello, famous for her "It's Lauren, Of Course!" videos, is my friend and mentor. Lauren introduced this citrus salad to me about ten years ago, and I think of her every time I prepare it. I find it refreshing at any hour of the day—and as an added bonus, it's an excellent source of vitamin C in the chill of winter.

ingredients

4 grapefruits

4 Cara Cara oranges

Arils (the red, shiny jewels inside that are often referred to as seeds) of 1 pomegranate

Handful fresh mint leaves

method

1. Zest 2 oranges and set aside.
2. Segment grapefruits and oranges so no pith remains on segments. Arrange fruit segments in large bowl. Squeeze the remaining juice from the citrus skins into bowl. Add pomegranate arils and mint and sprinkle reserved zest, if using, over all.
3. Serve chilled.

Reverse-Sear Steak with Sautéed Mushrooms + Roasted Rosemary Potatoes

Prep
5 m

Cook
45-60 m

Yield
4 servings

The reverse-sear method makes it easy to cook a steak that is nice and juicy on the inside and beautifully caramelized on the outside. When meat is cooked perfectly, I believe less is more. This recipe calls for simple seasoning and sautéed mushrooms—adding up to a melt-in-your-mouth steak entrée.

ingredients

4 New York strip steaks

4 teaspoons steak seasoning (I like "The Rub," by Second City Prime, available online and in select stores)

Few drizzles olive oil

Grapeseed oil, for searing

Sautéed Mushrooms and Roasted Rosemary Potatoes (recipes follow on p. 56), for serving

method

1. Place empty cast-iron skillet in lower rack of oven and preheat oven to 265°F.
2. Line a rimmed baking sheet with foil and place roasting rack on top.
3. Pat steaks dry. Drizzle few drops oil on each steak and rub oil on steak until coated, so seasoning sticks to meat. Repeat until all steaks are coated.
4. Sprinkle each steak with ½ teaspoon seasoning per side. Place steaks on prepared baking sheet.
5. Roast steaks 30 to 35 minutes (internal temperature should be 125°F for medium-rare doneness).
6. Remove steaks and skillet from oven carefully (use oven mitts). Lightly rub skillet with olive oil and place over medium-high heat on stove top.
7. Sear each steak in skillet 1 to 2 minutes per side, or until caramelized. Remove from heat and set aside to rest 10 to 15 minutes.
8. Serve hot topped with the Sautéed Mushrooms, and with the Roasted Rosemary Potatoes on the side.

Sautéed Mushrooms

Prep
5 m

Cook
5-7 m

Yield
4 servings

ingredients

2 tablespoons unsalted butter
2 tablespoons olive oil

16 ounces Baby Bella mush-rooms, sliced
2 teaspoons steak seasoning

method

1. In large sauté pan over low heat, warm butter and olive oil. Add mush-rooms and seasoning, raise heat to medium-high, and cook, stirring frequently, 5 to 7 minutes. Remove from heat.
2. Serve hot on top of steak.

Roasted Rosemary Potatoes

Prep
15 m

Cook
40 m

Yield
4 servings

ingredients

1½ pounds fingerling pota-toes, quartered
½ Vidalia onion, coarsely chopped
2 tablespoons olive oil

2 tablespoons minced fresh rosemary (about 4 large sprigs)
1 teaspoon sea salt
1 teaspoon freshly ground black pepper, to taste

method

1. Preheat oven to 400°F. Line rimmed baking sheet with parchment paper.
2. Toss potatoes with onion, olive oil, and rosemary in large mixing bowl. Sea-son with sea salt and black pepper.
3. Spread potatoes on baking sheet and roast, stirring halfway through cook-ing time, 40 minutes, or until golden brown. Remove from oven.
4. Serve hot with steak.

Cranberry Sauce

Prep
5 m

Cook
20 m

Yield
1 quart

Cranberry sauce is not just for Thanksgiving. Once, I served this as a garnish with my Ginger Soy Salmon (see p. 40), and another time, I served with the Reverse-Sear Steak (see p. 55) in place of the mushrooms. Both times, it was a big crowd pleaser. This relish can dress up any simple protein.

ingredients

1 (20-ounce) can crushed pineapple, drained

12 ounces fresh cranberries

½ cup water

Freshly grated zest and freshly squeezed juice of 1 orange

3 tablespoons date syrup (for a sweeter sauce, replace with pineapple juice)

1 cinnamon stick

½ teaspoon fennel seeds

½ teaspoon anise seeds

¼ teaspoon ground cinnamon

method

1. In small saucepan over medium heat, combine all ingredients and bring to a boil.
2. Reduce heat to low and simmer about 15 minutes. Remove from heat.
3. Serve warm, at room temperature, or chilled.

Sweet Potato Soup with Black Beans + Roasted Tomatoes

Prep
15 m

Cook
45 m

Yield
3 quarts

Soup and sweet potatoes are two of my favorite winter foods, so this Sweet Potato Soup is a winner for me! This soup is hearty and filling, but not rich—yet another healthy comfort food.

ingredients

4 sweet potatoes, peeled and cubed (about 3 pounds)

¼ cup olive oil

Pinch sea salt

Few grinds freshly ground black pepper

1 medium onion, chopped

1 carrot, peeled and chopped

2 celery stalks, chopped

2 quarts chicken stock

2 cans black beans, rinsed and drained

2 recipes (2 pints) Balsamic Roasted Tomatoes (see p. 35)

1 package Trader Joe's Sweet Apple Chicken Sausage, cut on the bias into ½-inch pieces

Chopped fresh flat-leaf parsley, for garnish

method

1. Preheat oven to 425°F. Line baking sheet with parchment paper.
2. Toss sweet potato cubes in large bowl with 3 tablespoons olive oil and season with sea salt and black pepper.
3. Transfer to prepared baking sheet and roast 20 minutes. Remove from oven.
4. While sweet potatoes are roasting, in stockpot over medium-low heat, warm 1 tablespoon olive oil. Add onion and sauté 10 minutes. Add carrot and celery and sauté 5 minutes.
5. Add roasted sweet potatoes and stock, raise heat to medium-high and simmer, uncovered, 20 minutes. Remove from heat.
6. Using immersion blender or powerful blender, puree soup until smooth.
7. Warm dry non-stick sauté pan over medium heat. Add sausage pieces and quickly fry until browned on each side. Remove from heat and set aside.
8. Add black beans, balsamic roasted tomatoes, and chicken sausage to pureed soup. Serve garnished with parsley.

Rice Noodle Salad with Peanut Dressing

Prep
15 m

Yield
4 servings

Just looking at this rainbow of vegetables puts a smile on my face. The peanut dressing and the rice noodles were inspired by my favorite Thai foods.

ingredients

1 cup grapeseed oil

½ cup freshly squeezed orange juice + more, as needed, to thin dressing

½ cup smooth peanut butter

¼ cup tamari soy sauce

3 tablespoons sesame oil

2 tablespoons roughly chopped fresh ginger

2 tablespoons rice wine vinegar

2 garlic cloves, roughly chopped

1 (1-pound) package rice noodles, cooked or soaked per package instructions

1½ cups shredded purple cabbage

1 carrot, peeled and shredded

1 red bell pepper, seeded and julienned

1 cup sugar snap peas

2 celery stalks, sliced

2 scallions, thinly sliced

⅓ cup cilantro leaves, for garnish

Salted or unsalted peanuts, for garnish

Sesame seeds, for garnish

method

1. Process grapeseed oil, orange juice, peanut butter, tamari soy sauce, sesame oil, ginger, rice wine vinegar, and garlic in powerful blender until smooth. Set aside.

2. Layer rice noodles and all vegetables on a platter or evenly divide among individual bowls.

3. Drizzle with the peanut dressing and garnish with cilantro, peanuts, and sesame seeds. Serve at room temperature or chilled.

Tomato Basil Dill Soup with Grilled Cheese

Prep
15 m

Cook
1 h 5 m

Yield
2½ quarts

Tomato soup and grilled cheese reminds me of when I was a kid as it was my favorite camp lunch. This classic is always satisfying and warms my mood on a cloudy day.

ingredients

2 tablespoons olive oil

2 tablespoons unsalted butter

1 yellow onion, finely diced

2 carrots, peeled and finely diced

2 celery stalks, finely diced

1½ teaspoons sea salt

1½ teaspoons freshly ground
   black pepper

Pinch crushed red pepper flakes
   (taste before adding more, as it
   gets spicy quickly)

6 cups chicken or vegetable
   stock

1 (28-ounce) can chopped San
   Marzano tomatoes with juice

2 tablespoons chopped fresh dill

2 tablespoons chopped fresh
   basil leaves

Grilled Cheese sandwich (recipe
   follows on page 66), for serving

method

1. In stockpot over medium-low heat, warm olive oil and butter. Add onion and sauté, stirring often, about 10 minutes, until onion is translucent and golden brown. Add carrots and celery and sauté 8 minutes. Add sea salt, black pepper, and red pepper flakes and sauté, stirring constantly, 2 minutes.

2. Raise heat to medium-high, stir in stock and tomatoes with juice, and bring to a boil.

3. Reduce heat to low and simmer, uncovered and stirring occasionally, about 45 minutes. Remove from heat.

4. Using immersion blender or powerful blender, puree soup. Stir in dill and basil just before serving. Serve hot with Grilled Cheese sandwich.

Grilled Cheese

Prep
2 m

Cook
4-5 m

Yield
1 serving

ingredients

1 teaspoon unsalted butter or olive oil

2 slices sourdough bread

2–3 slices cheddar cheese

method

1. Spread butter or olive oil on outside of both bread slices. Place cheese in center of bread.

2. Toast sandwich in panini maker or on preheated griddle or cast-iron skillet for 4 to 5 minutes, until cheese melts and bread has nice grill marks. Remove from heat and serve hot.

Spring

Spring Asparagus Salad with Za'atar Vinaigrette

Prep
10 m

Cook
10 m

Yield
4 servings

To me, fresh asparagus is synonymous with springtime. It's so exciting to have new vegetables after a long winter hibernation, with limited seasonal ingredients. I love the contrast of zingy lemon juice with the aromatic za'atar seasoning in this salad's dressing.

ingredients

½ bunch asparagus

¼ cup olive oil + 1 teaspoon more, for roasting asparagus

1 teaspoon sea salt

1 teaspoon freshly ground black pepper

1 cucumber, seeded and chopped

½ cup cherry tomatoes, halved

½ (14-ounce) can quartered artichoke hearts, drained

½ (14-ounce) can hearts of palm, drained and sliced into rounds

1 bunch fresh basil leaves, torn into bite-size pieces

Freshly squeezed juice of 2 lemons (about ¼ cup)

1 tablespoon za'atar seasoning (this Middle Eastern spice is a combination of seasonings that often includes thyme, oregano, sumac, and sesame seeds; each area of the region has its own twist on this)

method

1. Preheat oven to 425°F. Line baking sheet with parchment paper.
2. Trim or snap ends off asparagus and arrange them on prepared baking sheet. Drizzle with 1 teaspoon olive oil and season with few pinches each of sea salt and black pepper. Roast in oven for 10 minutes. Remove from oven and set aside to cool.
3. Either serve asparagus as full pieces on a platter with remaining vegetables and basil leaves arranged separately or slice into bite-size pieces and combine with remaining vegetables and basil leaves in a bowl.
4. Whisk together lemon juice, ¼ cup olive oil, za'atar, and remaining sea salt and black pepper and pour over salad. Serve immediately.

Turkey BLt Salad with Caesar Dressing

Prep
10 m

Yield
4 servings

This simple salad is a unique twist on the classic BLT. It's perfect for a crowd, because it takes minutes to prepare, and just about everyone loves a Caesar salad.

ingredients

**for the dressing
(makes 2½ cups)**

1 cup freshly grated parmesan cheese

½ cup vegan mayonnaise (Vegenaise) or regular mayonnaise

Freshly grated zest and freshly squeezed juice of 2 lemons

¼ cup olive oil

3 tablespoons anchovy paste (about 1 [2-ounce] tube)

3 garlic cloves, minced

1 tablespoon Worcestershire sauce

2 teaspoons Dijon mustard

1 teaspoon freshly ground black pepper

for the salad

1 head romaine lettuce

8 cooked turkey bacon slices

½ pint cherry tomatoes, halved

Freshly shaved parmesan cheese, for garnish

1 package bread sticks, for serving

method

1. Make dressing: Combine grated parmesan cheese, mayonnaise, lemon juice and zest, olive oil, anchovy paste, garlic, Worcestershire sauce, Dijon mustard, and black pepper in powerful blender and blend until smooth. Set aside.
2. Make salad: Divide romaine lettuce, tomatoes, and turkey bacon equally among 4 plates.
3. Drizzle 2 tablespoons dressing over each plate.
4. Garnish with shaved parmesan cheese and serve with bread sticks.

Hummus Beet Tortilla

Prep
5 m

Yield
2 servings

Sometimes I'm craving a fast, filling snack or lunch, but I want something more interesting than a sandwich. My Hummus Beet Tortillas do the trick every time, and you'll taste that they're packed with surprising flavors you usually find in salads.

ingredients

½ cup store-bought hummus

4 corn tortillas, lightly toasted

1 cup arugula

1 avocado, sliced

1 beet, spiralized

Crumbled goat cheese, for garnish

Candied pecans (I prefer Trader Joe's brand), for garnish

method

1. Spread 2 tablespoons hummus on each tortilla. Top each with equal amounts arugula, avocado, and beet.
2. Garnish each with equal amounts goat cheese and candied pecans. Serve immediately.

Yogurt Bowl with Strawberry Rhubarb Compote

Prep
15 m

Cook
20 m

Yield
1 yogurt bowl + 2 cups compote

Strawberry rhubarb pie is always a favorite during the late spring and early summer months. Why not turn that same idea into breakfast? This simple compote is perfect with plain Greek yogurt.

ingredients

for the compote

1 pound strawberries, rinsed, hulled, and chopped (about 2 cups)

½ cup granulated sugar

1 tablespoon freshly squeezed lemon juice

2½–3 cups chopped rhubarb

2 tablespoons water

for the yogurt bowl

2 tablespoons compote

½ cup plain Greek yogurt

1 dash ground cinnamon

½ banana, sliced

¼ cup Almond Cherry Granola (see p. 88)

¼ cup sliced strawberries

1 tablespoon chia seeds

1 tablespoon goji berries

method

1. Make compote: In small saucepan over medium heat, combine strawberries, ¼ cup sugar, and lemon juice. Cook, stirring continuously, about 3 minutes, until fruit softens. Remove from heat. Remove strawberries with slotted spoon to separate bowl and set aside to cool. Reserve strawberry juice in saucepan.

2. In another small saucepan over medium-low heat, combine rhubarb, remaining sugar, and water and cook until simmering. Cook, stirring constantly as it simmers, 5 minutes, until rhubarb softens. Remove from heat. Remove rhubarb with slotted spoon to bowl of strawberries.

3. Return saucepan with strawberry juice to medium-low heat and cook 10 minutes, until thickened and reduced by about half. Add cooked strawberries and rhubarb to pan and remove from heat.

4. Use warm or store in airtight container and refrigerate to serve cool.

5. Make yogurt bowl: Stir together compote, yogurt, and cinnamon in serving bowl. Top with banana, Almond Cherry Granola, strawberries, chia seeds, and goji berries. Serve.

Spinach + Strawberry Salad with Mint Lime Vinaigrette

Prep
15 m

Yield
6 servings

Strawberries and spinach are at their peak in the springtime. We planted our spinach seeds in April, and the dark, leafy greens were ready to be harvested in only a month. Come May, our spinach had grown into such beautiful and vibrant bunches that we decided to take our photos of this salad smack dab in the middle of the garden.

ingredients

for the dressing

Freshly grated zest and freshly squeezed juice of 4 limes

½ cup olive oil

2 tablespoons finely chopped fresh mint leaves

2 tablespoons honey

Pinch sea salt

Few grinds freshly ground black pepper

for the salad

8 cups fresh spinach leaves

2 Granny Smith apples, thinly sliced

1 cup strawberries, rinsed, hulled and sliced

½ cup pecan halves

½ cup crumbled goat cheese

Handful whole fresh mint leaves, for garnish

method

1. Make dressing: Combine lime zest and juice, olive oil, finely chopped fresh mint, honey, sea salt and black pepper in a Mason jar with a tightly fitted lid. Shake until dressing is emulsified.

2. Make salad: Combine spinach leaves, apple slices, and strawberries in a serving bowl and lightly drizzle dressing over top. Toss until all leaves are well coated.

3. Top with pecans and goat cheese.

4. Garnish with whole fresh mint leaves and serve.

Arugula Salad with Fava Beans, Burrata, + Smoked Salmon

Prep
15 m

Cook
1 m

Yield
4 servings

Fava beans have a mild, grassy flavor that's reflective of spring. In this salad, the sweet, tender legume is counterbalanced with peppery arugula leaves. Serve this dish with a toasted bagel or crisp French bread any time of the day.

ingredients

1 pound fava beans (after cooking, should yield 1 cup beans)

Water, as needed

1-2 teaspoons sea salt for boiling water + 1 pinch for seasoning

¼ cup olive oil

Freshly grated zest and freshly squeezed juice of 1 lime

1 tablespoon finely chopped fresh mint leaves

Few grinds freshly ground black pepper

4 cups arugula

1 pound thinly sliced smoked salmon

2 radishes, thinly sliced

2 (4-ounce) balls burrata cheese

1½ teaspoons fennel seeds, toasted, for garnish

1½ teaspoons caraway seeds, toasted, for garnish

1 lemon, sliced, for garnish

method

1. Remove fava beans from pods by tearing off ends and pulling down on string-like seams. Discard strings, ends, and pods.
2. Place large bowl of ice water in sink.
3. Bring large pot of water to a boil. Add 1-2 teaspoons sea salt.
4. Drop beans into pot and cook 1 minute. Immediately remove from heat, drain, and transfer beans to ice water (this stops the cooking process and keeps the beans a bright green color). Set aside to cool completely.
5. Remove thick skin covering each bean by breaking open skins and squeezing them out.
6. Whisk together olive oil, lime zest and juice, mint, remaining pinch sea salt, and black pepper. Set aside.
7. Arrange arugula on a platter. Top with fava beans, smoked salmon, radishes, and burrata. Drizzle dressing over top.
8. Garnish with toasted fennel and caraway seeds and lemon slices and serve.

Rigatoni with Broccoli, Cherry Tomatoes, Arugula, + Buffalo Mozzarella

Prep
10 m

Cook
12 m

Yield
4-6 servings

This colorful pasta dish came together on an evening when my house was filled with company and my guests asked for a tour of the vegetable garden. The broccoli, arugula, and basil were all ready for harvest and everyone was hungry, so voilà! This was a true crowd pleaser.

ingredients

2 teaspoons sea salt

1 pound dried rigatoni

3 cups broccoli florets

2 tablespoons unsalted butter

2 tablespoons olive oil

¼ teaspoon freshly ground
   black pepper

Pinch red pepper flakes

1 pint cherry tomatoes, halved
   and seasoned with a pinch
   each of sea salt + freshly
   ground black pepper

1 cup arugula

⅓ cup freshly grated
   parmesan cheese

8 ounces buffalo mozzarella
   cheese, torn into bite-size
   pieces

¼ cup chiffonaded fresh basil
   leaves, for garnish

method

1. Bring 6 quarts of water to a boil. Add 1 teaspoon sea salt and dried rigatoni to water. Stir gently and return to a boil. Boil, uncovered, 9 minutes. Add broccoli and boil 3 minutes. Remove from heat and drain. Set hot pot aside.

2. Add butter, oil, remaining sea salt, black pepper, and red pepper flakes to empty hot pot. Mix in pasta and broccoli, arugula and stir in cherry tomatoes and parmesan cheese. Top with buffalo mozzarella.

3. Garnish with basil and serve.

Kale Salad with Lemon Basil Buttermilk Ranch Dressing + Breadcrumbs

Prep
15 m

Cook
5 m

Yield
4 servings + 2½ cups dressing

Lemon basil is my absolute favorite variety of the herb. It has a bright, citrusy flavor that is sweeter than traditional basil. The lemon basil gives the buttermilk ranch dressing an extra punch and tastes delicious with raw kale. The dressing recipe makes about 2½ cups of dressing, so you'll have plenty left over to use in other salads.

ingredients

1 bunch kale (about 4 cups once ribs removed and chopped)

Freshly squeezed juice of 2 lemons, juiced separately

2 slices sourdough bread, toasted

1 cup vegan mayonnaise (Vegenaise) or regular mayonnaise

½ cup buttermilk

½ cup plain Greek yogurt

½ cup fresh lemon basil leaves, densely packed

1 scallion, white parts only, thinly sliced

1 tablespoon Dijon mustard

1 tablespoon basil olive oil (can be purchased online or at an oil & vinegar store)

1 teaspoon sea salt

1 teaspoon freshly ground black pepper

½ cup freshly grated parmesan cheese

Few purple chive blossoms, for garnish

method

1. Tear kale leaves off ribs and discard ribs. Chop leaves and soak in cold water; drain and spin in salad spinner to dry.
2. Massage shredded kale with juice of 1 lemon. Refrigerate in sealed, non-reactive container in refrigerator for up to 1 week.
3. Preheat oven to 400°F.
4. Place toasted bread in food processor and pulse into bread crumbs. Scatter bread crumbs on baking sheet and toast again in oven for 5-7 minutes (being careful not to burn). Remove from oven.
5. Make dressing: Combine remaining lemon juice, mayonnaise, buttermilk, Greek yogurt, lemon basil, scallion, Dijon mustard, basil olive oil, sea salt, and black pepper in powerful blender and puree until smooth. (Dressing can be refrigerated in an airtight container for up to 5 days.)
6. Toss kale, bread crumbs, parmesan cheese, and ½ cup of dressing or more to coat entire salad. Garnish with chive blossoms, if using, and serve.

Açai Bowl

Prep
5 m

Yield
1 serving

My daughter loves açai bowls but doesn't always want to eat first thing in the morning. This packs beautifully in a glass jar and travels well. I find the unsweetened açai packets have the perfect level of sweetness, and the cacao powder adds a smooth, chocolatey flavor.

ingredients

1 (100-g) packet frozen unsweetened açai berries

½ banana (preferably frozen)

1 date, pitted and chopped into tiny pieces

2 tablespoons almond milk

1 tablespoon almond butter

1 tablespoon cacao powder

¼ cup Almond Cherry Granola (recipe follows on p. 88)

¼ cup fresh blueberries

1 tablespoon unsweetened coconut flakes

1 tablespoon chia seeds

1 tablespoon goji berries

method

1. Run açai berry packet under cool water, open packet, and break into pieces before placing in powerful blender. Add banana, date, almond milk, almond butter, and cacao powder to blender and puree until smooth.

2. Pour into shallow bowl and top with Almond Cherry Granola, blueberries, coconut flakes, chia seeds, and goji berries. Serve.

Almond Cherry Granola

ingredients

3 cups rolled oats

1 cup sliced almonds

1 cup unsweetened
  coconut flakes

¼ cup flax seeds

2 tablespoons ground
  cinnamon

1 teaspoons sea salt

⅓ cup brown sugar

⅓ cup maple syrup

⅓ cup coconut oil

2 teaspoons vanilla extract

1 egg white

¾ cup unsweetened
  and unsulfured dried
  cherries

method

1. Preheat oven to 300°F. Line rimmed baking sheet with parchment paper.
2. Thoroughly mix together oats, almonds, coconut flakes, flax seeds, cinnamon, and sea salt in large bowl and set aside.
3. In small saucepan over low heat, stir together brown sugar, maple syrup, and coconut oil until sugar dissolves. Remove from heat and stir in vanilla extract.
4. Fold contents of saucepan into oat mixture and stir until all ingredients are well coated.
5. In separate bowl, beat egg white until stiff. Gently fold into granola mixture.
6. Pour granola onto prepared baking sheet. Bake 35 to 40 minutes, stirring once halfway through baking process, until dry, lightly toasted, and golden. Remove from oven and set aside to cool.
7. Once cool, add dried cherries. Use immediately or store in airtight container at room temperature up to 1 month.

Summer

Grilled Peaches, Heirloom Tomatoes, + Burrata Salad

Prep
10 m

Cook
10 m

Yield
4 servings

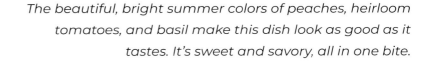

The beautiful, bright summer colors of peaches, heirloom tomatoes, and basil make this dish look as good as it tastes. It's sweet and savory, all in one bite.

ingredients

Grapeseed oil, for preparing grill

2 peaches, halved

2 heirloom tomatoes (any variety), sliced

Few pinches large-flake sea salt

Few grinds black pepper

8 ounces burrata cheese

Handful fresh basil leaves

method

1. Preheat grill to medium heat. Oil grill and flesh side of peaches before placing peaches on grill. Grill 8 to 10 minutes, until peaches have nice grill marks. Remove from grill.
2. Layer tomato slices on a plate and season with sea salt and black pepper.
3. Break up burrata cheese into chunks.
4. Top tomato slices with grilled peaches, burrata chunks, and basil leaves, and serve.

Kohlrabi Red, White, + Blue Salad

Prep
15 m

Yield
4 servings

Kohlrabi (also known as turnip cabbage) tastes like the offspring of a radish and jicama; the re-freshingly crisp, juicy vegetable is loaded with vitamin C. Matchsticks of kohlrabi and the fresh garden flavors of fennel, dill, and seasonal berries come together in this light, bright salad. The red strawberries, white kohlrabi, and blueberries are perfect for a Fourth of July picnic.

ingredients

½ cup fresh blueberries

½ cup hulled fresh mini strawberries

2–3 tablespoons balsamic vinegar

1 large kohlrabi bulb, peeled and cut
    into matchsticks or shaved into
    thin slices (about 2 cups)

½ cup thinly sliced celery

1 scallion, white part only, finely sliced

2 tablespoons chopped fennel stalk
    and frond

2 tablespoons chopped fresh dill

Freshly grated zest and freshly
    squeezed juice of 1 lime

Few pinches sea salt

Few grinds freshly ground black
    pepper

method

1. In small bowl, marinate berries in balsamic vinegar and set aside.

2. In large bowl, combine kohlrabi, celery, scallion, fennel stalk and frond, and dill. Mix in lime juice and zest. Season with sea salt and black pepper.

3. Pour balsamic berries over salad. Garnish with dill and/or fennel fronds. Serve.

take a short cut: Prep kohlrabi and celery and toss in lime juice 1 day ahead; refrigerate until ready to use.

think out of the ice box: Substitute strawberries and blueberries with raspberries and blackberries.

Herbed Tuna Salad

Prep
15 m

Yield
2 cups

Tuna salad is a standby anytime it seems like there's no food in the house. In the midst of summer, when the garden is filled with fresh herbs, this staple can be dressed up for lunch at a moment's notice.

ingredients

2 (5-ounce) cans albacore tuna in water, drained

½ cup finely chopped celery stalks

¼ cup thinly sliced scallions

2½ tablespoons mayonnaise or Vegenaise

2 teaspoons Dijon mustard

2 teaspoons red wine vinegar

1 teaspoon finely chopped dill fronds

½ teaspoon finely chopped fresh tarragon leaves

1½ teaspoons finely chopped fresh lemon basil leaves

1½ teaspoons finely chopped fresh Thai basil leaves

Few grinds freshly ground black pepper

1–2 pinches sea salt

Salad or bread, for serving

method

1. Mix all ingredients together in a bowl.
2. Serve with salad or as a sandwich on bread.

Seeded Pizza with Kale Pesto + Beets

 Prep
2 h

 Cook
30 m

 Yield
3 pizzas

This garden pizza is full of surprises, with the bright flavor of Kale Pesto (inspired by True Food Kitchen) shining atop an herbed crust. I use arugula and beets for my toppings, but this pizza would be delightful with any in-season vegetable. For best results, use a pizza stone.

ingredients

for the pizza dough

1 tablespoon active dry yeast

1 teaspoon sugar

1 cup warm water (110°F or less)

2½ cups all-purpose flour + more for dusting

3 tablespoons olive oil

1 teaspoon sea salt

1 teaspoon each anise, caraway, coriander, cumin, and fennel seeds, crushed

for the pizza

¾ cup Kale Pesto (see Savory Greek Yogurt with Kale Pesto recipe, p. 113)

3 beets, blanched, peeled, and thinly shaved

1½ cups fresh arugula

3 cups shredded mozzarella cheese or mozzarella sticks

method

1. Make pizza dough: In a large bowl, dissolve yeast and sugar in warm water. Allow yeast mixture 10 minutes to bloom. *You will know it's ready when the top of the mixture looks frothy.*

2. Mix in flour, olive oil, sea salt, and crushed seeds to yeast mixture. Knead on a floured surface for a few minutes, until dough comes together. Add more flour, 1 tablespoon at a time, if dough is too sticky; add more olive oil if dough is too dry. Place dough in greased bowl and set aside to rise 2 hours or until doubled in size.

3. Place pizza stone in oven and preheat oven and stone to 450°F.

4. Knead dough and divide it into 3 equal pieces. Roll out each piece into shape of pizza stone. Place dough rounds on parchment paper.

5. Spread ¼ cup Kale Pesto over each dough round. Top each with equal portions beets, arugula, and cheese.

6. Using a pizza peel, transfer 1 pizza on parchment paper at a time to hot pizza stone and bake 12 minutes, or until cheese is golden brown. Remove from oven with peel and repeat baking with other pizzas. Slice and serve hot.

Strawberry Scallion Quinoa

Prep
10 m

Cook
6 m

Yield
6 servings + ½ cup dressing

Strawberry Scallion Quinoa screams summer. I gather the sweet strawberries and fresh celery, scallions, and herbs for this recipe directly from my garden. This dish is full of bright summery flavors, including my absolute favorite herb, lemon basil.

ingredients

1 pound fresh strawberries, hulled and cut in half

2 tablespoons balsamic vinegar

1 (8-ounce) package halloumi cheese

Grapeseed oil, for preparing grill

Freshly grated zest and freshly squeezed juice of 1 lemon

6 tablespoons olive oil

2 tablespoons champagne vinegar

½ teaspoon sea salt

½ teaspoon ground black pepper

1 cup cooked quinoa

⅓ cup chopped fresh mint leaves

⅓ cup chopped fresh flat-leaf parsley

⅓ cup fresh lemon basil, sliced into chiffonade

⅓ cup finely chopped celery

6 scallions, white part only, chopped (about ¼ cup)

1 cup halved pecans

method

1. In small bowl, marinate strawberries in balsamic vinegar and set aside.
2. Cut halloumi cheese into ¼-inch-thick slices.
3. Preheat grill to medium heat. Oil grill and halloumi slices before placing cheese on grill. Grill 3 minutes, until cheese begins to melt and get nice grill marks. Turn and repeat on other side. Remove from grill and cut into long, thin strips.
4. Whisk together lemon juice and zest, olive oil, champagne vinegar, salt, and black pepper. Set aside.
5. In large bowl, mix together quinoa, mint, parsley, lemon basil, celery, and scallions. Pour in dressing and toss again.
6. Drain strawberries from marinade and arrange them over quinoa. Top with pecans and grilled halloumi cheese slices and serve.

Rainbow Chard Turkey Wrap

Prep
5 m

Yield
1 serving

Cut the carbs and load up on vitamins and minerals by wrapping up some turkey in a big, brightly colored leaf or two of rainbow chard. I love the fresh flavors and cheerful colors of the herbs and veggies in this wrap.

ingredients

1 tablespoon mayonnaise or Vegenaise

1 teaspoon finely chopped tarragon leaves

¼ teaspoon Dijon mustard

1–2 large rainbow chard leaves

3 ounces roasted turkey, sliced

1 tablespoon shredded beet

1 tablespoon shredded carrot

3 sprigs fresh cilantro

method

1. In small bowl, mix mayonnaise or Vegenaise with tarragon leaves and Dijon mustard.
2. Spread tarragon sauce evenly across rainbow chard leaves. Layer chard leaves with turkey, beet, carrot, and cilantro. Roll up chard, forming a wrap, and serve.

Caramelized Beets with Honey'd Lavender Rosemary Ricotta

 Prep
10 m

 Cook
30 m

Yield
4–6 servings

Beets are one of those love-it-or-hate-it vegetables, but I believe this dish will make a convert out of any beet naysayer once they taste it. This Honey'd Lavender Rosemary Ricotta can be paired with fruits or vegetables alike; it all depends on whether you're craving something sweet or savory.

ingredients

4 medium beets, peeled and quartered or cut into eighths (about 2 cups of ½-inch pieces total)

¼ teaspoon sea salt

¼ teaspoon freshly ground black pepper

1 tablespoon olive oil, for roasting beets

1 pound ricotta cheese

2 tablespoons finely chopped fresh lavender + 1 extra sprig, for garnish

2 tablespoons finely chopped fresh rosemary + 1 extra sprig, for garnish

1 tablespoon honey, warmed until it is thin

1 tablespoon balsamic vinegar

1 tablespoon chopped toasted walnuts

method

1. Preheat grill to medium-high heat (about 450° degrees F).
2. Place beets on sheet of foil large enough to fold into a packet. Season beets with a sea salt, black pepper, and 1 tablespoon each of chopped rosemary and lavender. Drizzle with olive oil.
3. Fold foil packet closed and grill packet 25 to 30 minutes. You will know the beets are done when they are easily pierced with a fork. Remove from grill.
4. In large bowl, mix together ricotta cheese, 1 tablespoon each of chopped lavender and rosemary, and honey. Spread mixture on a plate.
5. Top with roasted beets and walnuts. Drizzle balsamic vinegar over top, garnish with lavender and rosemary sprigs, and serve.

Grilled Peaches with Honey'd Lavender Ricotta

Prep
10 m

Cook
10 m

Yield
4 servings

This version of peaches and cream looks beautiful on the plate and tastes heavenly. It's perfect on a hot summer night.

ingredients

Grapeseed oil, for grilling

4 peaches, halved

1 pound ricotta cheese

1½ tablespoons finely chopped fresh lavender

1 tablespoon honey, warmed until it is thin

½ cup fresh raspberries

1 tablespoon chopped fresh mint leaves

method

1. Preheat grill to medium-high heat. Rub hot grill grates with grapeseed oil.
2. Lightly oil flesh side of peaches. Grill 8 to 10 minutes, or until peaches have nice grill marks and are cooked.
3. In large bowl, mix together ricotta cheese, lavender, and honey. Spread mixture on a plate.
4. Top with grilled peaches, raspberries, and mint, and serve.

Chocolate Cherries with Honey'd Lavender Ricotta, Macadamia Nuts, + Graham Cracker Crumbs

Prep
10 m

Cook
10 m

Yield
6 servings

I made this dessert for a dinner party on a whim. It's fun to share on a platter and dip graham crackers or a spoon right in it. It may not win a contest for prettiest dish on the table, but after a nice meal and a few glasses of wine, just close your eyes and enjoy the flavors!

ingredients

1½ cups red cherries, pitted and halved

½ cup dark chocolate chips

1 pound ricotta cheese

1 tablespoon fresh lavender, finely chopped

1 tablespoon honey, warmed until it is thin

1 cup graham cracker crumbs

½ cup macadamia nuts

method

1. Preheat grill to medium-low heat.
2. Using aluminum foil, make a small packet and wrap cherries and chocolate chips in packet. Place on grill. Roast on grill about 10 minutes, or until cherries are cooked and chocolate is melted.
3. In large bowl, mix together ricotta cheese, lavender, and honey. Spread mixture on a plate or divide evenly into 6 tall glasses.
4. Layer ricotta mixture with chocolate cherries, graham cracker crumbs, and macadamia nuts, and serve.

Black Beans with Broccoli, Rainbow and Swiss Chard, + Goat Cheese

Prep
15 m

Cook
15 m

Yield
6 servings

The brilliant-colored leafy greens of both Swiss and rainbow chard are so inviting. This dish just sort of happened one summer day after I harvested the garden and wanted to do more than just sauté a few chard leaves. The black beans add a rich heartiness to this vibrant dish.

ingredients

Olive oil, for sautéing

1 onion, chopped

¼ teaspoon sea salt + a few pinches for additional seasoning

¼ teaspoon freshly ground black pepper + few pinches for additional seasoning

1 small bunch broccoli florets, cut into pieces

3 Swiss chard leaves and stems, chopped

3 rainbow chard leaves and stems, chopped

1 tablespoon ground cumin

1 (15-ounce) can black beans, drained and rinsed

½ cup roughly chopped fresh cilantro leaves

1 lime, halved

Crumbled goat cheese, for garnish (optional)

method

1. In Dutch oven over medium heat, warm 1 to 2 tablespoons olive oil until wavy. Add onion, season with a pinch each of sea salt and black pepper and sauté, stirring constantly, about 5 minutes.
2. Add broccoli and chard leaves and stems to onions. Season with ¼ teaspoon each of sea salt and black pepper, and cumin and stir until well combined. Cook 3 minutes.
3. Stir in black beans and cook for 1 minute, or until beans are warmed through. Remove from heat.
4. Mix in cilantro leaves, squeeze lime halves over dish, and garnish with goat cheese crumbles, if using. Serve.

Savory Greek Yogurt with Kale Pesto

Prep
5 m

Yield
1 serving + 2 cups Kale Pesto

Savory yogurt bowls take just a few minutes to assemble but keep you satisfied for hours. If you want to change up your lunchbox routine, put this in a Mason jar and you're good to go.

ingredients

for the kale pesto

8 cups stemmed and
    chopped kale
1 cup grated parmesan
    cheese
¾ cup olive oil
½ cup pine nuts
4 garlic cloves, minced
2 teaspoons sea salt
Pinch red pepper flakes

for the yogurt

1 cup plain Greek yogurt
¼ cup halved cherry
    tomatoes
¼ cup fresh blackberries
½ avocado, pitted and
    sliced
1 tablespoon Kale Pesto
Handful chopped
    walnuts
Pinch sea salt
Olive oil, for drizzling

method

1. Make pesto: Bring large pot of water to a boil. Fill large bowl with ice cubes and cold water.
2. Add kale to boiling water and blanch 3 minutes. Using tongs or slotted spoon, remove kale from water and submerge 3 minutes in ice bath to shock (stops cooking process and maintains bright green color).
3. Remove kale from ice bath and squeeze out excess water.
4. Place kale, parmesan cheese, olive oil, pine nuts, garlic, sea salt, and red pepper flakes in food processor and puree until smooth.
5. Make yogurt: Place yogurt in bowl and add cherry tomatoes, blackberries, avocado, Kale Pesto, and walnuts. Sprinkle with sea salt and drizzle with olive oil. Serve.

think out of the ice box: To make Lemon Basil Pesto, simply substitute the kale with 5 cups fresh lemon basil and jump right to step 4 (no need to blanch).

Greek Salad

Prep
15 m

Yield
4–6 servings

My twist on the Greek Salad is straight outta' the garden. This is a such a simple salad, yet it is brimming with varied flavors and textures: an array of vegetables, olives, and feta cheese topped with a tangy oregano vinaigrette. This salad paired with Quinoa Tabbouleh (see p. 116) makes a perfect summer meal that can easily be packed into Mason jars and taken along for a picnic.

ingredients

for the dressing

½ cup good olive oil

¼ cup good red wine vinegar

2 cloves garlic, minced

1 tablespoon finely chopped fresh
   oregano leaves

1 teaspoon sea salt

½ teaspoon Dijon mustard

½ teaspoon freshly ground black pepper

for the salad

1 head romaine lettuce, torn into bite-size
   pieces

1 cucumber, thinly sliced

1 tomato, thinly sliced

1 red pepper, seeded and julienned

1 cup kalamata olives, pitted

1 cup crumbled feta cheese

1 scallion, white part only, thinly sliced

method

1. Make dressing: Place all ingredients in glass jar with tight-fitting lid and shake until emulsified.
2. Make salad: In large salad bowl, layer all ingredients.
3. Drizzle dressing over salad and serve.

Quinoa tabbouleh

Prep
15 m

Cook
15 m

Yield
6 servings

Quinoa tabbouleh is one of my daughter's favorite dishes that I prepare. The crunch of the cucumbers, the tang of the tomatoes, and the pronounced flavors of mint and scallion make this a bold dish on its own. Since quinoa is a good source of protein, this can easily be served as an entrée, but it's also light enough to be served as grain dish in a multi-course meal.

ingredients

1¼ cups water

1 cup quinoa, rinsed well

1 teaspoon + pinch sea salt

½ teaspoon freshly ground black pepper

Freshly squeezed juice of 2 lemons

1 bunch scallions, white part only, chopped (about ½ cup)

¼ cup olive oil

1 clove garlic, minced

1 cucumber, seeded and chopped

1 pint cherry tomatoes, halved

1 bunch fresh flat-leaf parsley, roughly chopped (about 1 cup)

1 bunch fresh mint leaves, roughly chopped (about 1 cup)

method

1. In medium saucepan over high heat, bring water, quinoa, and pinch sea salt to a boil.
2. Reduce heat to medium-low, cover, and simmer 10 minutes, or until quinoa is tender. Remove from heat and let stand, covered, 5 minutes.
3. Fluff quinoa with a fork.
4. In small bowl, whisk together lemon juice, scallions, olive oil, and garlic. Season with remaining 1 teaspoon sea salt and black pepper. Set aside.
5. In large bowl, combine quinoa, cucumber, tomatoes, parsley, and mint.
6. Drizzle dressing over contents of bowl and stir all ingredients together. Serve.

Garden Tomato Bread Soup

Prep
5 m

Yield
6 (1-cup) servings

Saladette tomatoes are little orange garden tomatoes that are somewhat larger than a golf ball but smaller than a tennis ball. One late August, my garden was overflowing with saladettes, so my mom asked me to create this soup as a flavorful reminder of her recent trip to Tuscany. You can find these sweet, juicy delights—or something similar—at your local farmers market in late summer.

ingredients

28 ounces saladette tomatoes, roughly chopped (be sure to weigh them, because homegrown tomatoes vary in size)

4 cups sourdough breadcrumbs (toast sourdough bread slices and crumble in a food processor to make breadcrumbs)

3 garlic cloves, minced

2 scallions, white parts only, chopped

1–3 cups water or stock

2 teaspoons sea salt

2 teaspoons freshly ground black pepper

Few pinches crushed red pepper

6 tablespoons Lemon Basil Pesto (see note on Savory Greek Yogurt with Kale Pesto recipe, p. 113), for garnish

Shredded parmesan cheese, for garnish

method

1. Combine tomatoes, breadcrumbs, garlic, scallions, and 1 cup water in powerful blender. Season with sea salt and black pepper and puree until smooth. Add up to 2 cups more water to achieve desired consistency.

2. Transfer contents of blender to individual serving bowls. Garnish each serving with 1 tablespoon Lemon Basil Pesto and sprinkle of parmesan cheese.

3. Warm contents of blender in a pan over low heat and serve or serve at room temperature.

Index

About the Authors

Nicole

NICOLE PUTZEL is a classically trained chef, recipe developer, cooking instructor, and author of the cooking blog PUTZELKITCHEN.com. She is dedicated to cooking and sharing healthy, seasonal food made from scratch from her organic vegetable garden.

Claudia

CLAUDIA CHOCANO is a Peruvian photographer and medical Spanish interpreter who also holds degrees in psychology and holistic health coaching. She believes that good nutrition directly affects our mental and physical well-being, and that it is crucial for prevention of future disease.

Photo credit: Karla Livney